T0079143

FLASHBACK TO THE . . .

FLY '90s

BY Patty MichaeLs   ILLustRated by SaRah RebaR

Ready-to-Read

SIMON SPOTLIGHT
An imprint of Simon & Schuster Children's Publishing Division
New York London Toronto Sydney New Delhi
1230 Avenue of the Americas, New York, New York 10020
This Simon Spotlight edition May 2023
Text copyright © 2023 by Simon & Schuster, Inc.
Illustrations copyright © 2023 by Sarah Rebar • Stock photos by iStock
For information about special discounts for bulk purchases, please contact Simon & Schuster Special Sales at 1-866-506-1949
or business@simonandschuster.com.
Manufactured in the United States of America 0323 LAK
2 4 6 8 10 9 7 5 3 1
Library of Congress Cataloging-in-Publication Data
Names: Michaels, Patty, author. | Rebar, Sarah, illustrator.
Title: Flashback to the . . . fly '90s / by Patty Michaels ; illustrations by Sarah Rebar.
Description: Simon Spotlight edition. | New York : Simon Spotlight, an imprint of Simon & Schuster Children's Publishing Division, 2023. | Series: Flashback | Audience: Ages 5 to 7 | Summary: "Let's go back in time to the . . . 1990s, where "grunge" music and clothing were all the rage, Lunchables and Crystal Clear Pepsi were packed in your lunch box, and a strange thing called the "Internet" was just about to take over the world. Kids will love learning so many things about the '90s in this lighthearted, entertaining, and informative Ready-to-Read filled with fun photos, illustrations, and facts about some of the coolest things to have happened during that decade. Topics in this book include: popular toys and trends like collecting Beanie Babies; must-see preschool TV like Barney and The Teletubbies; and off-the-wall food trends (Crystal Clear Pepsi, anyone?); fashion and fads like grunge and '90s dance crazes; and technology and communication like pagers, cordless phones and the birth of the Internet. A fun '90s themed activity will be included in the backmatter"— Provided by publisher. Identifiers: LCCN 2022036931 (print) | LCCN 2022036932 (ebook) | ISBN 9781665933506 (hardcover) | ISBN 9781665933490 (paperback) | ISBN 9781665933513 (ebook) Subjects: LCSH: Nineteen nineties—Juvenile literature. Classification: LCC D856.M53 2023 (print) | LCC D856 (ebook) | DDC 909.82/9—dc23/eng/20220830
LC record available at https://lccn.loc.gov/2022036931
LC ebook record available at https://lccn.loc.gov/2022036932

GLOSSARY

Caller ID: A phone service that shows you the number of the person calling you

Call-waiting: A phone feature that notifies you with a beep when another person is trying to call you while you're currently talking on the phone

CD (compact disc): A small disc containing music or data

Doc Martens: A popular brand of boot-style footwear

Electric Slide: A group dance performed to the song of the same name typically done at weddings and parties

Grunge: A genre of music that reached its height of popularity in the 1990s, incorporating other styles of music, like punk rock and heavy metal

Iconic: A word that means "widely known"

Macarena: A Spanish dance based on a song of the same name

Pager: A small, portable electronic device that beeps or vibrates when someone is trying to reach you

Personal computer (PC): A multipurpose computer designed for individual people to use

Tamagotchi: A small, egg-shaped toy with a screen, containing a digital pet to take care of

Wicked: Another word for "great" or "exceptional"

Note to readers: Some of these words may have more than one definition. The definitions above match how these words are used in this book.

CONTENTS

Chapter 1
Off-the-Chain Trends

Are you ready for an amazing time-traveling adventure?
We are going way back . . .
to the fly 1990s!

Lace up your **Doc Martens** as you learn about fabulous fads, fresh trends, and other majorly cool things that helped define the decade.

Toys in the '90s were off the hook. Kids loved Beanie Babies, **Tamagotchis** (say: Tam-AH-GOT-chees), Furbies, and Tickle Me Elmo. The store Build-A-Bear Workshop debuted in 1997, letting kids make their own unique stuffed animals!

The Beanie Babies craze began in 1995. The first nine Beanie Babies included a frog, a pig, a lobster, and a platypus!

And home video-gaming systems got more modern with the launch of Nintendo 64 and Sony PlayStation. Sony PlayStation used **CDs** instead of cartridges for its games, which provided *super* high-quality graphics.

CDs were also replacing the way
people listened to music.
Stores like Sam Goody, FYE,
and Tower Records were the
coolest places to check out
CDs from the newest bands.

The first song to ever use
Auto-Tune as a sound
effect came out in 1998.

Grunge music was popular,
and so were other types,
such as rap, hip-hop, pop,
and music from teen bands.
And everyone was learning new dances
like the **Macarena** and the **Electric Slide!**

When kids weren't listening to the dopest music, they were watching popular '90s TV shows like *Teletubbies*, *Rugrats*, *Barney & Friends*, and *The Powerpuff Girls*.

And anyone who grew up in the 1990s will remember TGIF, which stood for Thank Goodness It's Funny. Families gathered on the couch on Friday nights to watch comedy shows like *Full House* and *Family Matters*.

You might hear people say "TGIF!" That phrase also means "Thank Goodness It's Friday!"

Food and snacks in the '90s were totally **iconic** (say: eye-CON-ick). Kids couldn't wait to pack Lunchables in their backpacks and have Hot Pockets and Bagel Bites after school.

Funyuns and Dunkaroos were some other popular snacks. And who didn't love a cold and clear Crystal Pepsi to wash it all down?

3D Doritos were introduced in 1998 and were recently re-released in 2020!

Chapter 2
Super-Fresh Fashions and Fads

Fashions and fads of the 1990s were pretty **wicked**.
People weren't just listening to grunge music, they were getting inspired to dress in a grunge style, too.

Grunge fashion trends included flannel shirts, ripped jeans, graphic T-shirts, and **Doc Martens**.

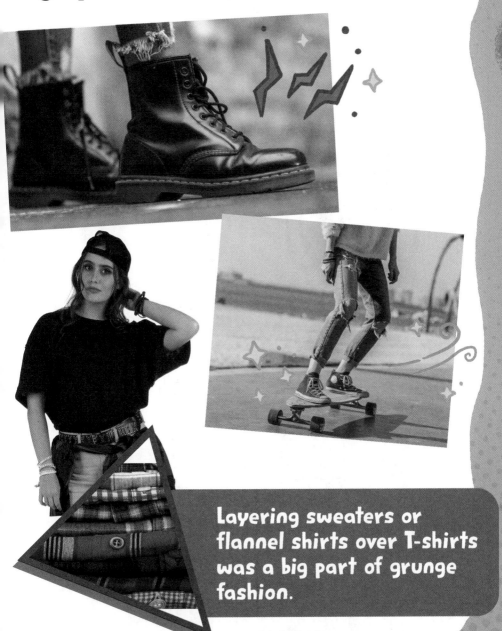

Layering sweaters or flannel shirts over T-shirts was a big part of grunge fashion.

If grunge wasn't your style, you might have been rocking another popular look of the decade: cargo pants with a bucket hat.

wow!!

Cargo pants were first developed by the British military in 1938.

Another favored trend of the decade was wearing bold colors and patterns, especially geometric patterns and shapes.

Hairstyles of the '90s were *all that* and a bag of chips. Popular styles included pixie cuts, bobs, baby bangs, big curls, flattops, cornrows, and chin-length waves.

Layered hairstyles were all the rage in the '90s. Popular TV shows had characters with layered haircuts, and soon you could see that style everywhere.

Everyone loved accessories
like choker necklaces,
tiny butterfly clips, fanny packs,
and sneakers with pumps in them.
And who didn't have their backpacks
and school supplies decorated
with the colorful art style
of Lisa Frank?

Chapter 3
You've Got Mail!

When it comes to the 1990s, nothing changed more than methods of communication.

A **pager** was the coolest device to let you know someone wanted to get in touch with you. And **caller ID** and **call-waiting** on landlines became popular. Now you were not only able to see who was calling you, but also put a call on hold to take another call!

Before call-waiting, if you dialed someone who was already on the phone, you'd hear a busy signal.

Personal cell phones were also becoming more popular.
They were more affordable and smaller than when they were first invented.

A cell phone style known as the "flip phone" was *the* item to have in the '90s.

Popular movies of the '90s started showing characters using cell phones, adding to their popularity!

More and more people started owning **personal computers** (or **PCs**) in the '90s. And many people started using portable PCs (called "laptops").

CDs in the 1990s weren't just used for playing music or video games. Computer programs in the '90s also ran on CDs. CDs also started to phase out floppy disks for data storage.

And the reason why personal computers were becoming so widespread? All because of a little method of communication known as . . . the World Wide Web!

According to statistics from 2022, 63 percent of the world's population uses the Web!

The World Wide Web is an internet
system that allows users to
search for information.
In the 1990s it became available
in homes, libraries, and cafés
across the United States.
People started to "surf the Net"
to look up all sorts of information and
send emails instead of "snail mail"!

Another shift in technology was the creation of AOL (America Online). It was one of the biggest internet service providers in the United States in the 1990s.

AOL was one of the very first companies to tap into the community of the internet, with instant messaging, buddy lists, and online gaming.

In order to access the internet, people would have to dial into the service by using a phone line!

Wasn't that a super-fly
look back at the 1990s?

Now that you know a little about
what was popular in the 1990s,
can you name some things
from that decade that are similar today?
What things are completely different?

Memories in the Making!

Here's a fun 1990s-based activity that'll give you even more insight into this defining decade. Ask a grown-up who lived in the 1990s what their life was like. Did they have a pager or a cell phone? What were their favorite TV shows, and what did they like to wear? And can they describe what the internet was like when it was really just beginning?